The 2020 Presidential Election is undoubtedly, the most important election of the century. Amid an onslaught of senseless killings among unarmed African Americans by vigilante civilians and trigger-happy police and a pandemic which unveiled an enormous disparity in health care for African Americans, the country is being led by an incumbent Commander in Chief who appears "unbothered" by it all. In November, America is tasked with choosing its next leader--one who will be charged with salvaging what's left of its Democracy. And once again, African Americans are at the forefront of each candidate's mind, which is typical. Our role in the establishment of wealth and power in America began in August 1619, with the arrival of the first twenty slaves from Angola African, yet, we have been perpetually exempt from any of the benefits. Now, more than ever, a complete understanding of our role as stakeholders in the political process is crucial-- and the Southern Strategy is a great place to start.

Sincere thanks to Dr. Eric Grant, SFC Thomas Parks, my Arifjan (Kuwait) family and my family back home in the states, for your perspectives and your patience.

Love you Zeth Blaimes!!!

Knowledge is power; however, the implementation of knowledge empowers...

"You start out in 1954 by saying 'nigger, nigger, nigger'. By 1968, you can't say 'nigger' – that hurts you. Backfires. So you say stuff like, uh, forced bussing, states' rights and all that stuff. You're getting so abstract now you're talking about cutting taxes, and all these things you're talking about are totally economic things and a byproduct of them is blacks get hurt worse than whites. And subconsciously maybe that is part of it. I'm not saying that. But I'm saying that if it is getting that abstract, and that coded, that we are doing away with the racial problem one way or the other. You follow me – because obviously sitting around saying 'We want to cut this' is much more abstract than even the bussing thing, and a hell of a lot more abstract than 'nigger, nigger, nigger...'"
Lee Attwater, Republican Strategist (Nixon)

"Democrats have always had the African American vote..." President Donald Trump 2018
This statement; by America's forty-fifth President, could not be further from the truth.

"Blind Democrat" is a term that is frequently used to describe African American voters. Extreme right-winged Conservatives use the term to imply that little to no thought is used when it comes to choosing political candidates in the African American community. Ironically, African Americans are also criticized for "abandoning the Republican Party"; when in fact, the slow transition to the Democratic Party was an act of necessity due to the Republican Party's unwillingness to support the advancement of the former slave. On the national level (presidential elections) Republicans can easily win without the African American vote. As a result, African American initiatives are not a priority for Republican candidates—the GOP's purposeful exclusion of African Americans from their political agenda is well-known. However, the concomitant impassiveness and sense of entitlement

from Democratic politicians places African American voters at the mercy of the Democratic Party. Within the one-party system, the greatest disadvantage for African Americans is the fact that the Democratic Party can count on our votes without being held accountable for their actions or inactions on our behalf. *This is in spite of the fact that the Democratic Party has not won a Presidential election without the African American vote since World War II.* This, in and of itself, is the basis for Trump's assertion that African Americans are *"blind Democrats"*. Again, this is far from the truth. —we are not blind. Our voting actions are driven by the well-documented behavior of a political system that was created before we were considered human beings...we're simply playing the hand that we were dealt. In the author's opinion, now is a good time to "reshuffle".

With regard to the subject matter of this work—why is the information relevant today? The primary purpose of this work is two-fold: to provide a brief and chronological overview of America's political system as it relates to African American voters and to facilitate the creation of a political strategy that will maximize the impact of the African American voter and the accountability of politicians. In order for the political process to work in our favor, we have to participate at all levels. We can no longer vote in Presidential elections—without voting in elections at the state and local levels—and expect the system to work. Our lack of participation in the 2010 midterm election is a prime example of the devastating outcome. Sadly, we played right into the hands of the extreme right-winged arm of the Republican Party. In 2010, Senate Republican leader Mitch McConnell of Kentucky famously declared *"the single most important thing for the GOP was to make President Obama a one-term president"*. While McConnell was unable to accomplish this goal, gerrymandering and other forms of electoral manipulations created a polarized congress. Republicans adopted a simple, systematic plan to resist anything President Obama proposed —and it worked. To be clear, the power of the President is not absolute. Our lack of participation created a precarious situation for the sitting President—one that is akin to a soldier who has a weapon without ammunition.

With further regard to the impassiveness of the Democratic Party over the years, the resultant effect is the disenfranchisement and subsequent indifference to the political system among African Americans—particularly young African Americans. The 2016 Presidential election is an important demonstration of the impact. Because of the relationship with the Republican Party and the lack of enthusiasm for Hilary Clinton, an overwhelming number of African Americans opted to forgo participation in the election completely. As a result, Donald Trump is now the 45th President.

The 2016 election is a demonstration of power and unity in its purest form and should be the blue print for African Americans in the re-strategizing of our political position as stakeholders in the political process, as opposed to simply **"blind Democrats"** as Trump so eloquently implied.

In closing—we only represent 13% of the population; however, the impact of the African American vote is still undeniable—**especially when cast or withheld in unity.**

INTRODUCTION TO SLAVERY IN AMERICA

Prior to the Pilgrims' landing at Plymouth in 1620, the first English colony was established in Jamestown Virginia in 1607. Slow acclimation to the environment, poor water supply, and a lack of food resulted in the deaths of many of the original colonists. The harsh conditions coupled with the lack of experienced laborers further complicated the transition to the new world. The remedy was the acquisition of labor, first from the Native Americans (1670-1730). Slavery quickly evolved to become the economic and social backbone for the new world and slave ownership symbolized wealth and prosperity.

Native American Slaves
Slavery was not a foreign concept to the Native Americans; however, there were a number of differences related to the manner of practice. In the Native American culture, race was not a primary factor in determining which tribes to enslave, as evidenced by the fact that the Natives enslaved their own for various reasons. However, perceived inferiority did play a role in the selection process. Thus, upon the invasion of North America by the European settlers, the "divide and conquer" methodology was easily applied. "Inferior tribes" were initially sold to the Europeans by other tribes. The division among tribes

would eventually lead to the demise of the Native Americans. Comparatively, the same methodology was used by the Europeans in the acquisition of African slaves from various African tribes. With regard to the treatment of Native American slaves, many European settlers were ambivalent about the enslavement of Native Americans. Comparatively, the enslavement of Native American and African slaves was held differently in the minds of the Europeans; and as a result, the bondage of the Native American slave was often "redeemable". In contrast, African slaves were not redeemable.

The Irish Slavery Myth

Contrary to the revisionist's account of slavery in America, the Irish were never held in perpetual captivity, nor were they ever considered sub-human. Recent attempts to equate the indentured servitude of the Irish with the African slave experience is totally false and should be debunked once and for all. While the Irish have been subjected to human bondage throughout history, they were never held considered "chattel" or property. And though some were sentenced to indentured servitude in the "new world," a majority of Irish indentured servants came voluntarily and many would go on to become slave owners themselves.

August 1619

Most historians agree that the arrival of West African slaves to the American colonies occurred on August 20,

1619. An unofficial number of men, women and children departed Angola, destined for Mexico. After being captured by pirates, the Portuguese slave ship arrived in Jamestown, Virginia carrying "20 or so Negroes". After surviving the treacherous voyage, these individuals were put to work in the tobacco fields. Unbeknownst to them, this was the proverbial beginning of the end of freedom for over 12 million human beings of African descent. Endorsed by the European colonies, the institution of forced labor defined by race and class, was created to fulfill the needs of the settlers. Unlike the Native American slaves and the indentured servants from Ireland, the bondage of the African slave would last for 246 years. In addition to the duration of captivity, the stark difference in the manner of treatment of the African slaves was painfully obvious.

Chattel Slavery
African slaves were held and defined legally as "chattel" or items of property other than real estate. They were considered devoid of emotion and lacking in the ability to feel physical pain. In essence, enslaved Africans were considered sub-human. They worked for free and received only the basic necessities to sustain life. The end result was the expansion of wealth for Europeans and the creation of wealth for settlers in the new world, which remains to this very day and is enjoyed by the descendants of slave owners. In contrast, the descendants of slaves have yet to recover from the psychological, emotional, and economical damages of slavery.

The Constitution's Reference to Slavery
"While some members of the Constitutional Convention voiced eloquent objections to slavery, they consented to a document which laid a foundation for the tragic events which were to follow."
Thurgood Marshall

The words "slave" or "slavery" were not mentioned in the ***Articles of the Confederation and Perpetual Union***, which was adopted in 1781 as the original governing document of the United States. It was America's first Constitution. Within this document, the power to regulate slavery was implicitly left to the individual colonies. This is not surprising considering the position of the esteemed leaders of the time. Thomas Jefferson referred to slavery as a "hideous blot" on America and George Washington, an owner of 100 slaves, described it as "repugnant". Benjamin Franklin (a former slaveholder) and Alexander Hamilton (who was born in a slave colony in the British West Indies) went on to become members of anti-slavery societies. Because of the negativity surrounding the immoral and dehumanizing act of slavery, the subject was conveniently and consciously ignored by the authors of the country's governing document. Although slavery was the primary source of survival and wealth in America, they recognized the stain and the legacy of hypocrisy that it created.

T he Constitutional Convention of 1787
The Articles of the Confederation were adopted by Congress in 1777; however, it would take an additional four years for ratification by the states. The Articles created a loose coalition of sovereign states and a weak central/federal government, which left most of the power with the state governments. Ongoing division among the states concerning a number of issues; to include excessive land taxation, high legal costs, economic depression and slavery, eventually threatened to negate the purpose of the Revolutionary War. Addressing the laws within the original document seemed to be the most viable solution. During the Constitutional Convention of 1787, the Articles of the Confederation were revised to further define the plan for governing the United States.

T he 3/5 Compromise
During the convention, the issue of slavery resulted in a bitter debate. South Carolina proposed the prohibition of federal involvement in the regulation of the Atlantic Slave Trade. Luther Martin, a slaveholder from Maryland stated that slavery was "inconsistent with the principles of the Revolution," and "dishonorable to the American character." A Virginia delegate, George Mason, argued "every master of slaves is born a petty tyrant...They bring the judgment of heaven on a country."

A delegate from South Carolina countered that religion and humanity have nothing to do with slavery and *"unless regulation of the slave trade was left to the states, the southern-most states shall not be parties to the union."* Clearly, the conflict regarding slavery was a threat to the Union nearly a century before the Civil War.

Congressional representation was at the center of the debate. In their quest for power, the Southern states realized that the inclusion of the enslaved in their census would increase their political power tremendously. Delegates from the North objected to this because the measure was profoundly hypocritical in light of the fact that the enslaved could not vote, own property or enjoy any of the privileges of their owners. Ironically, the hypocrisy of the proposed measure and the morality-based discomfort regarding the institution of slavery among Northern lawmakers did not compel them to advocate for the emancipation of the enslaved. In the end, the Northern lawmakers ignored their personal issues concerning the immorality of slavery for fear that the Southern states would not join the Union.

In spite of the significant role that slavery played in the formation and progression of the Union, the terms "slave" or "slavery" were still left out of the Constitution. *"Protection of private property"* as prescribed by the Constitution, subliminally prohibited the federal and state governments from abolishing slavery. Against the best wishes of the founding fathers and many others, the Constitution substantially strengthened the institution of slavery in America, effectively making it a ***"proslavery document"***. On the other hand, it established the power by which the federal government could eventually abolish slavery. The immediate plan for representation and the distribution of power was the ***3/5 Compromise***. The founding fathers agreed that the distribution of power should be based on population. Each state would receive delegates in the House of Representatives and the Electoral College accordingly. According to the compromise, each state was given one representative for every 30,000 people in the House of Representatives and two representatives in the Senate. ***They agreed to count enslaved Africans as three-fifths of a person for "taxation and representation" purposes,*** giving the Southern states more electoral power. The measure laid the groundwork for the exploitation of African Americans in the political process, which continues to this day.

Crisis in the Democratic Party
Due to the political advantage in the South that was created by the Electoral College and the 3/5 Amendment, the Democratic Party was the dominant party in the United States for 28 years (1828-1856), losing only two elections during this timeframe. Internal differences stemming from the Northwest Ordinances of the 1780s; which prohibited the expansion of slavery to the Western territories, caused a division between Northern Democrats and Southern Democrats. Once again, the issue of slavery threatened to destroy the Union. Southern Democrats advocated for slavery in all territories, while Northern Democrats proposed that each territory should decide individually. The split in the party would ultimately result in the election of Republican candidate Abraham Lincoln in 1860. He won without the support of any of the Southern states. The election of 1860 established the two party system that exists today and set into motion events that would eventually give rise to America's Civil War. While several theories concerning the origins of the Civil War exist, most agree that the secession of the first seven states from the Union was the triggering event. But why did the initial seven states secede? The answer to this question is indeed the most sensible explanation for the actual cause of the war.

A Divided Union and the Rise of the Grand Old Party (GOP)
The Republican Party's opposition to the expansion of slavery in the West and their reason for the opposition was well known. The expansion of slavery into the newly formed territories would strengthen political power in the South even further. As a result, attempts to maintain a balance of power

within the Union were met with additional compromises and acts of Congress. (**See Missouri Compromise of 1820 and the Kansas-Nebraska Act**).

In 1854, opposition to the Kansas-Nebraska Act led to the joining of forces between a number of anti-slavery parties and disgruntled Northern Democrats. The joining of forces would eventually lead to the formation of the Republican Party. *While its foundational platform was anti-slavery, the goal of the Republican Party was not to abolish slavery in the South. The goal was to prevent the westward expansion of slavery, which would lead to the continued political dominance enjoyed by the South.*

P resident Lincoln and the Civil War
The election of Abraham Lincoln posed an immediate threat to the livelihood of Southerners, which was built on the institution of slavery. Immediately after the election, all seven states of the Deep South (Alabama, Florida, Georgia, Louisiana, Mississippi, South Carolina, and Texas) seceded from the Union. They were joined by the four states of the upper South (Arkansas, North Carolina, Tennessee, and Virginia) on April 12, 1861, when the firing on Fort Sumter signaled the beginning of the Civil War.

President Lincoln's position on slavery is confusing to many, to say the least. During his bid for the presidency, Lincoln argued that the founding fathers' assertion that, "All men are created equal" applied to all regardless of race. However, Lincoln's overall interpretation of this ideology was narrowly defined and did not reflect the concept in its entirety because it excluded social and political rights for individuals of African descent. As the President of the United States, Lincoln's decision to fight was based upon his desire to *prevent the secession of the Southern states and ultimately to save the Union*. It was his duty.

To further understand President Lincoln's position on slavery as it relates to the secession of the Southern states and the initiation of the Civil War, it is extremely important to note once again that the **preservation of the Union was the main objective.** To be absolutely clear, the Civil War and subsequent emancipation of the enslaved by President Lincoln should not be considered solely as an act of altruism. In fact, President Lincoln made this perfectly clear on at least two occasions...

"While I was at the hotel to-day an elderly gentleman called upon me to know whether I was really in favor of producing a perfect equality

between the negroes and white people. [Great laughter.] While I had not proposed to myself on this occasion to say much on that subject, yet as the question was asked, I thought I would occupy perhaps five minutes in saying something in regard to it. **I will say then that I am not, nor ever have been in favor of bringing about in any way the social and political equality of the white and black races,** *[applause]---that I am not nor ever have been in favor of making voters or jurors of negroes, nor of qualifying them to hold office, nor to intermarry with white people; and I will say in addition to this that there is a physical difference between the white and black races which I believe will forever forbid the two races living together on terms of social and political equality.* **And inasmuch as they cannot so live, while they do remain together there must be the position of superior and inferior, and I as much as any other man am in favor of having the superior position assigned to the white race."** *Abraham Lincoln September 18, 1858*

And again, in a response to an open letter to the New York Tribune that questioned his position on emancipation....

"My paramount object in this struggle is to save the Union, and is not either to save or to destroy slavery. *If I could save the Union without freeing any slave I would do it, and if I could save it by freeing all the slaves I would do it; and if I could save it by freeing some and leaving others alone I would also do that. What I do about slavery, and the colored race, I do because I believe it helps to save the Union; and what I forbear, I forbear because I do not believe it would help to save the Union. I shall do less whenever I shall believe what I am doing hurts the cause, and I shall do more whenever I shall believe doing more will help the cause. I shall try to correct errors when shown to be errors; and I shall adopt new views so fast as they shall appear to be true views."* **Abraham Lincoln August 22, 1862**

After the war, Lincoln was faced with the challenge of bringing harmony to the Union and finding a place in society for African Americans. Unfortunately, he lacked a clear plan. During a visit to Louisiana in April 1865, he proposed a plan that would include the provision of voting rights to some African Americans but not all— only those who had fought for the Union. He was assassinated three days after giving the speech.

Post Civil War-Reconstruction

The purpose of Reconstruction was the reintegration of the Southern states and the integration of 4 million formerly enslaved men, women and children into the Union.

After Lincoln's assassination, the task fell into the hands of the Vice President, Andrew Johnson. Johnson had been chosen to run on the Republican ticket because he was a Democrat and the Republicans wanted to prevent a loss for Lincoln after Civil War. They temporarily changed the name of the party to the "National Union Party" to attract anti-slavery Democrats and other anti-slavery sympathizers. An alleged "sympathetic slave owner" from Tennessee himself, Johnson had freed his slaves in 1863, while at the same time persuading Lincoln to exempt the state of Tennessee from the Emancipation Proclamation. Johnson was also a self-proclaimed Jacksonian Democrat who fought tirelessly for pro-slavery rights in the South; however, he did not consistently vote with either the Democrats or the newly formed Whig Party—which would eventually become the Republican Party. Johnson's chameleon attitude toward slavery and other legislative issues, created the appearance of a perfect candidate for such troubling times. The strategy worked and the Lincoln-Johnson ticket won by a landslide in the 1864 Presidential election. After Lincoln's assassination, Johnson's true feelings regarding the disposition of the former enslaved was immediately revealed. His overall plan for Reconstruction was rooted in **'states' rights'**, which would decrease the federal government's influence over the provision of rights to the former enslaved. Under Johnson's leadership, Southern legislators were given free rein to rebuild their states. Restrictive "Black Codes" were passed to control the movement and behavior of the former enslaved and other African Americans. In addition to this, all of the land that had been confiscated by the Union Army and given to the former enslaved, was given back to the former owners. The end result was limited freedom for the former enslaved and a virtually free labor force, as sharecropping became the new way of life.

By 1868, Johnson's continued efforts to resist all actions pertaining to the betterment of African Americans solidified his racist position and ultimately led to the first Presidential impeachment in American history. Nine articles of impeachment were applied, one of which was the "disgracing of Congress". Though the impeachment was not confirmed by the Senate, Johnson's actions regarding the disenfranchisement of the former enslaved were less severe in the aftermath of the impeachment process. However, the damage had already been done.

Radical Reconstruction 1867-1877

The **Radical Republicans** represented a sector of the Republican Party that strongly opposed slavery and the disenfranchisement of African Americans. They also sought to hold the Southern states fiscally and morally responsible for the Civil War, to include punishment for Confederate leaders.

The establishment of the Freedman's Bureau and passage of other Civil Rights legislation in 1866 established assistance for the former enslaved and defined all persons born in the United States as national citizens. The measures were quickly vetoed by President Johnson. In response to this action, Congress set out to make amendments to the Constitution. In 1867 they approved the expansive Fourteenth Amendment, which prohibited states from denying equal rights to all. The second part of the Amendment provided for a reduction in the number of state representatives if the right to vote was denied to the former enslaved. In the end, Southern leaders were given an ultimatum—discontinue the disenfranchisement of the former enslaved or lose congressional representation.

In 1867, Congress established a military Reconstruction program to enforce political and social rights for African Americans in the South. Under Radical Reconstruction, African Americans flourished and for the first time could conceptualize hope for a better life. African Americans held political offices, to include Governorships and Congressional seats. Louisiana elected its first African American governor, P.B.S. Pinchback in 1872 and there were a total of 600 African Americans who served as legislators. Unfortunately, old ways never really die.
Economically, African-Americans were still disadvantaged and found themselves competing with impoverished White Ameri-

cans for plantation jobs. Sharecropping, which was designed to perpetuate slavery, planted the seeds for generational poverty among African Americans. But poverty was not the greatest concern.

A product of deep-seated hatred, terrorist organizations such as the Ku Klux Klan (KKK), Knights of the White Camelia and the White Brotherhood disrupted political and social advances of the former enslaved. Through the use of terror; the self-proclaimed military arm of the Democratic South, systematically reduced the number of African American legislators and voters. Their purpose was to restore White supremacy to the South and they would eventually succeed. **(See Colfax Massacre and Coushatta Massacre-Louisiana).**

Presidential Election of 1876
The election of 1876 was hampered by voter corruption (ballot stuffing) and heightened violence in the Deep South. In the end, the election was decided by Congress, with Republican candidate Rutherford Hayes winning the election by one electoral vote. White Southern Democrats in the South agreed to accept Hayes' victory with an unwritten compromise. Among the list of demands by the South, was the removal of the remaining federal troops from the states still under military control (Louisiana and South Carolina) *and the "right to deal with Blacks without Northern interference".* Weary of rebellion, the terms were accepted and Reconstruction immediately came to an end. With no further protection from the North, the former enslaved lost the ability to exercise their freedom as citizens.

Post-Reconstruction

"The slave went free; stood a brief moment in the sun, then moved back again toward slavery."
W. E. B. Dubois

Empowered by resentment and hatred toward the federal government, White Southerners devised a plan to secure and maintain power in all local and state offices. Their efforts were effective due to the implementation of *"Jim Crow Laws"* which were an extension of the "Black Codes" that were utilized during the Reconstruction period. A segregated society rooted in White supremacy created an environment of second class citizenship and oppression for African Americans, which remain in a lesser regard to this very day. In the decade after the 1876 presidential election, the Republican led state governments in the South were replaced by former Confederates largely through voter suppression and terrorism. During this period, the priorities of the Republican Party shifted to economics and commercial matters, which strained their relationship with African American voters.

On the national level, the political picture was completely different. The 3/5 Compromise, which had established political power in the South, was now obsolete. However, voter suppression and the disenfranchisement of African Americans resulted in continued political dominance by
the Democratic Party on the state and local levels. Due to the same tactics, the Republican Party did not benefit from the African American vote in the South. Yet in spite of this, the office of the Presidency remained firmly in the hands of Republicans *due to the increased number of African American voters in the North.*

While political power in America was once determined by the institution of slavery in the South, it was now determined by the African American electorate in the North. To emphasize further, **whereas Southern states sought expansion of slavery to increase political power, the North fought against it for the same reason—*power.*** To be clear, the Civil War was indeed a result of the conflict over slavery; however, emancipation was not the main objective. Political power and the preservation of the Union were the primary objectives. According to Lincoln, the emancipation of the enslaved was purely "a tactic of war"...

The Great Depression (1929-1939)—The Transition of African Americans to the Democratic Party

The process began in the 1920s. By this time, Republicans consistently refused to pursue civil rights for disenfranchised African American voters. Northern Democrats, who supported the emancipation of the enslaved, only made subtle attempts to improve opportunities for African Americans. This became the catalyst for the realignment of political parties.

While the Great Depression served as the proverbial equalizer when it came to poverty and wealth in America, African Americans were hit the hardest, which is not a surprise. Prior to the market crash, African Americans were already disadvantaged due to lower wages and fewer job opportunities. The Great Depression worsened their condition as impoverished White Americans were given jobs once held by African Americans. As a result, the national unemployment rate for African Americans reached fifty per cent; but in places like Atlanta, Philadelphia and Detroit, it was sixty to seventy per cent.

Prior to the Great Depression, African Americans had remained loyal to the Party of Lincoln. However, the lack of support from Republican president Herbert Hoover after the market crash and his alignment with Southern segregationists was the triggering event for change—but change was not instant. During the Presidential election of 1932, sixty-five to seventy-five percent of the African American vote went to Hoover in the Northern states.

Again, this was primarily due to their loyalty to the Republican Party and an unwillingness to trust a Democratic candidate. In addition to this, Roosevelt's party affiliation (Democrat) and his stance on the issue of race during the campaign were also deterrents for African American voters. For example, to secure the Southern Democratic vote, Roosevelt opted not to advocate for the federal anti-lynching law, nor did he advocate for a ban on poll taxes that prevented African Americans from voting. In spite of the minimal support of African Americans, Roosevelt's strategy prevailed in the 1932 election. By 1936, the economic support that African Americans received under the New Deal resulted in a mass exodus to the Democratic party. Unfortunately, many of the economic advantages created by the New Deal were hampered by the fact that they were administered at the state level where systems of racism were stronger than ever. However, more African Americans were appointed to Roosevelt's administration than his Republican predecessors combined, and he tripled the number of African Americans employed by the federal government.

Democratic and Republican Parties 1932-1964

Founded in 1828 by Andrew Jackson, the Democratic Party promoted the expansion and continuation of slavery prior to the Civil War. In the aftermath of the Civil War and Reconstruction, the party strongly favored oppressive legislation to limit the civil rights of the former enslaved. From 1829-1860, the Andrew Jackson arm of the Democratic Party dominated the office of the Presidency, due mainly to the 3/5 Compromise and the electoral college. With the establishment of the Republican Party in 1860 and the subsequent Emancipation Proclamation; the electorate power structure that was sustained by the institution of slavery was removed. Out of loyalty, the Republican Party received the support of the former enslaved, ending the electoral advantage for the Democratic Party that was created by the institution of slavery.

From 1860-1932, the Republican Party consistently dominated the office of the Presidency. In the aftermath of the Great Depression, political power shifted once again. In addition to the African American vote, the New Deal coalition of the Democratic Party gained the support of recent European immigrants who were mostly Catholic. During this period From (1932-1964), the Democratic Party regained its dominance of the office of the Presidency, **without the support of Southern/Andrew Jackson Democrats.** This was also in spite of the voter suppression and continued disenfranchisement of African Americans, particularly in the Southern states. During this period, the Democratic Party had evolved to resemble the Republican Party that fought for the emancipation of the enslaved.

After the passage of the Civil Rights Act of 1964 and the Voting Rights Act of 1965, a complete realignment of both parties transpired, with Southern states consistently voting for Republicans and Northeastern states consistently supporting the Democratic Party. Beginning with the Presidential election of 1969, the Republican Party, which now resembled the Andrew Jackson Democratic Party of old, regained its dominance in the office of the Presidency. The question is—how?

SOUTHERN STRATEGY

*"From now on, the Republicans are never going to get more than 10 to 20 percent of the Negro vote and they don't need any more than that... but Republicans would be shortsighted if they weakened enforcement of the Voting Rights Act. **The more Negroes who register as Democrats in the South, the sooner the Negrophobe whites will quit the Democrats and become Republicans.** That's where the votes are. Without that prodding from the blacks, the whites will backslide into their old comfortable arrangement with the local Democrats..."* **Kevin Phillips, Nixon Political Strategist (1970)**

By definition, the Southern Strategy is a political tactic used by the Republican Party to maintain political power by appealing to racism—particularly against African Americans. As the civil rights of African Americans improved, and in the absence of Jim Crow legislation which impeded the African American voter, the Democratic Party was positioned to expand its political power. Ironically, this was reminiscent of the political dominance that was established with the passage of the 3/5 Compromise; **however, the current advantages for the Democratic Party were based on the promotion of freedom as opposed to oppression.** At the same time, Republicans had increasingly distanced themselves from all matters related to the betterment of African Americans and the "Party of Lincoln" was virtually extinct. For example, President Dwight Eisenhower (Republican) testified before Congress against integrating the military and criticized the landmark Brown versus the Board of education (1954), the Supreme Court decision that desegregated public schools. Clearly, the issue of race continued to be an important variable in the creation and sustainment of political power structures in America. Barry Goldwater and Richard Nixon are credited with using racism as a political strategy in the realignment of White conservative/Jackson Democrats to the Republican Party. With racism as the core principle of the Southern Strategy; states' rights, law and order, and evangelical Christianity are considered foundational principles as well.

Barry Goldwater

"I think we just delivered the South to the Republican Party for a long time to come..."
Lyndon Johnson after signing the Civil Rights Bill.

A retired General in the Air Force Reserves and Senator from Arizona, Barry Goldwater is the politician most often credited with the revitalization of American conservatism in the aftermath of the extremely liberal New Deal coalition. Prior to taking this position, Goldwater voted in favor of the desegregation of schools and supported the Civil Rights Bill of 1957. In 1964, he voted against the passage of the new Civil Rights bill, believing that too much power was given to the federal government. In addition to being a huge proponent of states' rights Goldwater was just as passionate about public safety and the enforcement of criminal justice/law and order.

Over the course of three years, Goldwater actively participated in the realignment of the Republican Party, which resulted in his nomination to run against Lyndon Johnson in the 1964 election. During the campaign, Goldwater used anti-Communism rhetoric, coupled with fear to appeal to racist Americans; particularly in the South. ***States-rights*** was one of the battle cries that evolved to become a euphemism for racial oppression.
After the hard-fought battle to win the Republican nomination for the 1964 Presidential election, Goldwater lost in a monumental landslide. But all was not lost. In the process, he garnered

record breaking support in the Deep South; and as a result, the Republican Party emerged as a new vehicle for White supremacy in the South.

Of note—Goldwater's inconsistent support of party issues is reminiscent of Andrew Johnson prior to his Vice Presidency.

Goldwater Trivia

- At the age of 16, Hillary Clinton campaigned for Barry Goldwater in 1964, although she was too young to vote.
She switched to the Democratic Party as a college student.

- Ronald Reagan was a staunch supporter of Barry Goldwater during the '64 election.

- During the '64 election, Strom Thurmond, the infamous segregationist from South Carolina, broke ties with the Southern Democrats (Dixiecrats) mid-race to join the Republican Party.

RICHARD NIXON

"The worst thing Richard Nixon ever did was to tell racists they had a point and welcome them into the party of Lincoln." **Richard Cohen Washington Post**

"You start out in 1954 by saying 'nigger, nigger, nigger'. By 1968, you can't say 'nigger' – that hurts you. Backfires. So you say stuff like, uh, forced bussing, states' rights and all that stuff. You're getting so abstract now you're talking about cutting taxes, and all these things you're talking about are totally economic things and a byproduct of them is blacks get hurt worse than whites. And subconsciously maybe that is part of it. I'm not saying that. But I'm saying that if it is getting that abstract, and that coded, that we are doing away with the racial problem one way or the other. You follow me – because obviously sitting around saying 'We want to cut this' is much more abstract than even the bussing thing, and a hell of a lot more abstract than 'nigger, nigger, nigger...'" **Lee Atwater, Republican Strategist** (Nixon)

While the Southern Strategy resulted in defeat for Barry Goldwater, the overall impact on the delivery of Southern Democrats to the Republican Party was resounding. However, it was not complete. During Goldwater's run for presidency, he failed to win the support of the most racist arm of the Democratic Party (Dixiecrats). Once a leader of the Dixiecrat Party, South Carolina segregationist, Strom Thurman, recognized the fact that party realignment was imminent after a loss in the Presidential election of 1948. During the '64 election, Thurmon made the transition to the Republican Party. Those left behind were the final remnants of the Jackson Party of Democrats. In an effort to gain their support, Nixon enlisted the help of Thurman's political strategist,

Harry Dent to perfect the Southern Strategy. According to Dent, **"kinder, gentler vocabulary of the new racial politics would deliver the White House to Republicans in five of the next six presidential elections"**.

Prior to his run for President in 1964, Nixon was a candidate in the 1960 election. In the '60 Presidential election against John F. Kennedy, Nixon entered the race as the candidate with more political ties to the African American community. While serving as Vice President during the Eisenhower administration, Nixon supported the Civil Rights Act of 1957. He also befriended Dr. Martin Luther King and frequently sought his advice. According to Dr. King, *"Nixon has one of the most magnetic personalities that I have ever confronted"*. Yet, in 1960, when Dr. King was jailed on a trumped up traffic charge, Vice-President Nixon failed to intervene publicly. Bobby Kennedy brokered the deal with the Justice Department for King's freedom. After this encounter, Dr. King stated, *"...when this moment came, it was like he had never heard of me...so this is why I really considered him a moral coward."*

Comparative to Andrew Johnson's chameleon approach to politics, Nixon's ability to appeal to both sides with sincerity was indeed a political gift— which earned him the monicker "Tricky Dick". **(It is important to note that "chameleon politics" were characteristic of the 4 Presidents who were considered for impeachment: Johnson, Nixon, Clinton, and Trump who was once a member of the Democratic Party before switching to the Republican Party in 1987. Since 1987, Trump has switched his party affiliation 5 times)**.

During the 1968 Presidential election, in a tactic now termed the *"political two-step,"* the Nixon administration was able "flip-flop" on several key issues while actively pursuing the White vote. For example, in the absence of the twenty-four hour news coverage that we have today, he used courtroom proceedings to quietly slow the desegregation of schools in the South to a snail's pace. His efforts were markedly contrary to his previous position on civil rights—while serving as Vice President during the Eisenhower administration, he supported the Civil Right's Act of 1957.

Another major difference between the Nixon/Goldwater campaign was Nixon's communication style. ***Through the use of coded language, signals, and political symbolism, he was able to speak directly to his political base*** in a manner that was less conspicuous when compared to Goldwater's appeal to Southern White Democrats. The phrase, ***"law and order" is an example of Nixon's use of euphemism to appeal to his base in the aftermath of city riots in 1967 and 1968. Today, the terminology is synonymous with the policing of African Americans.***

1972 PRESIDENTIAL ELECTION & WATERGATE

In addition to taking a $500,000 tax deduction, Nixon also owed capital gains taxes on a land deal in California. In 1970, he paid only $792.81 in federal income taxes and $878.03 in 1971, with an annual salary of $200,000. This in and of itself was not the reason for the burglary of the DNC Headquarters.

The reason for the break-in was two-fold—to find out if the DNC was aware of a relationship between Nixon and Howard Hughes and to conceal an illegal donation from Howard Hughes in the amount of $100,000. The money was spent on furnishings and jewelry for Nixon's family. Clearly, the administration was wrought with corruption and Nixon's demise was ultimately fueled by greed. **(Perspectively, financial transparency for the POTUS and any elected official is required to minimize the potential for negative influence and subsequent breaches to national security).**

The findings from the Watergate investigation led to the near impeachment of Nixon, with a total of three articles of impeachment imposed by the House of Representatives: obstruction of justice, abuse of power contempt of Congress. The bipartisan support of the Articles of Impeachment signaled a possible conviction by the Senate. On the advice of Senator Goldwater; after the release of the "smoking gun tapes," Nixon resigned.

Since the implementation of Nixon's Southern Strategy, only three Democratic Presidents have been elected to the White House versus six Republicans, to include Donald Trump.

THE REAGAN EFFECT

"To overcome this identity-based appeal, Republicans needed to resurrect old threats and manufacture news ones. They did both."
Angie Maxwell-Washington Post

To be clear, the "Southern Strategy" refers to the GOP's strategy to win national elections by appealing to the Southern states with White fear and racial resentment. But this is nothing new—race has played a role in America's power structure since the 3/5 Compromise in 1787. The Compromise, which in essence partially humanized the enslaved, established political dominance for the Southern Democrats, which lasted for nearly 30 years. Using race again as a polarizing agent, the GOP's realignment of Southern Democrats with the new Republican Party was completed in the '68 and '72 Presidential elections; however, complete dominance was not obtained. In 1976, the Democrats won the White House with Jimmy Carter—a White, born-again Southern Baptist peanut farmer. The question was how; since Southern Democrats had thoroughly embraced the race inspired platform of the GOP. To his credit, Carter's appeal was rooted in his ability to convey the fact that he was authentically one of them—a true Southern Democrat with Christian morals and conviction. Without a doubt, Nixon's demise played a role in Carter's success. After the 1976 election, the GOP was forced to acknowledge the imperfections in their strategy, as the country began to transcend racial stigmas and enter the realm of "post-racial" America.

"Recession is when your neighbor loses his job. Depression is when you lose yours. And recovery is when Jimmy Carter loses his."
Ronald Reagan

Ronald Reagan, "The Great Communicator", was the GOP's pick for the run against Jimmy Carter in 1980. Amidst a poor economy, record high unemployment and a hostage crisis in the Middle East, Reagan used his communication skills to persuade Southern Democrats to return to the GOP. His revision of Nixon's appeal to the Republican base via coded language included the introduction of terms like *"welfare queen"* which painted the Black woman as a free-loader and opportunist. And though he verbalized the need for colorblindness and the need to move past race, he openly blamed African Americans for their economic inequities. The overall impact was the creation of the notion that government programs, which were implemented to even the playing field for African Americans, were disadvantageous to White Americans.

Going a step further, other Reagan-era revisions to the Southern Strategy included an appeal to White evangelicals and a denouncement of feminism. His decision to forgo 40 years of support for the equal rights of women, and the politicizing of abortion and gay rights solidified the support of Southern White women and evangelicals for the GOP. The unwavering support of the two entities have resulted in numerous wins for the GOP.

And finally, his introduction of a tax-free income of $150,000, sealed the deal for the GOP. At the same time, it furthered the disenfranchisement African American voters, a few of which had remained loyal to the party of Lincoln. However, the loss of African the American vote, which was "written off" nearly fifty years ago, was not a major concern for the GOP, as predicted by Nixon's political strategist in 1970:

"From now on, the Republicans are never going to get more than 10 to 20 percent of the Negro vote and they don't need any more than that..."
Kevin Phillips, Nixon Political Strategist (1970)

The Republican Party's indifference to African American voters was even more profound during President Obama's tenure in the White House. This was due primarily to the establishment of a more conservative wing of the party, which was openly antagonistic to African American interests. The growth of this wing of the Republican Party is primarily responsible for the election of Donald Trump.

"With regard to the Southern Strategy, Goldwater discovered it; Nixon refined it; and Reagan perfected it...where does Trump come in..."
Ben Fountain, *The Guardian*

Nixon's successful implementation of the Southern Strategy and his ability to capitalize on the racial and cultural divisions of his day, opened the gate to the heightened political polarization that exists in the United States today. He also set the stage for the forty-fifth President of the United States. While President Donald Trump isn't an exact replica of Nixon, there is a distinct line that runs from Nixon's version of the Southern Strategy to Trump's version. In addition to this, corruption is a common theme for both administrations.

"The seeds of Trump's victory were sown the moment Obama won. This is White America's reaction to the death of the post-racial myth".
Joy Reid—Host, AM Joy

"Trump is at his core indecent. As a man, he's forever fledgling. Propped up by his wealthy father well into middle age, he struggles mightily with self-control, by his own admission fears self-reflection, and is clearly incapable of a range of human emotions, from empathy to humor. He has no use for tenderness, the arts, or spiritual pursuits. Trump traffics in debasement".
Noam Shpancer, Ph.D., *Psychology Today*

In the aftermath of the election of the nation's first African American president, Trump's decision to run for office was rooted in the concept of White supremacy. Prior to the Civil War, Lincoln alluded to the notion,
And inasmuch as they cannot so live, while they do remain together there must be the position of superior and inferior, and I as much as

any other man am in favor of having the superior position assigned to the white race."

To ensure a victory, Donald Trump doubled down on the Southern Strategy in 2016 to enhance his appeal to Southern voters and voters with an intolerance to race. This was not a surprise. However, Trump's obsession with the former President is quite disturbing and raises a number of unsettling questions. Overall, experts largely agree that Trump's obsession with President Obama is more egotistical than race related.

"Psychologically, we labor most to destroy that which is most threatening. And the most threatening is often what we most covet and can't have. When Trump sees Obama, he sees a truth that is both undeniable and untenable.
Trump needs Obama extinguished like darkness needs light extinguished—in order to exist."
Noam Shpancer, Ph.Psychology Today

In addition to widening the racial divide in his implementation of the Southern Strategy, Trump's continued appeal to the White evangelical population and the growing misogynistic ideals among the Republican base sealed the deal on his win against Hillary Clinton in 2016. In the aftermath of the victory, Trump's obsession with President Obama and his overt appeal to White supremacists have severely damaged race relations in America. *In fact, the polarizing leadership of the current administration poses a potential threat to the country in a manner that is reminiscent of the period immediately prior to the Civil War.*

Like his Republican predecessor decades earlier, campaign corruption has severely marred Trump's victory. Amid allegations of Russian interference with the election and inappropriate acts among cabinet members and others within his camp, impeachment proceedings prevailed against President Trump.
Unlike Nixon, who resigned before his impeachment due to congressional bipartisanship and a likely conviction, congressional bipartisanship was non-existent during the Trump impeach-

ment, with a Democratic House and a Republican Senate. Ultimately, the lack of bipartisanship would work in Trump's favor, as the Senate failed to bring forth a conviction.

TRUMP V/S NIXON

To say that Nixon and Trump were both unscrupulous politicians is an accurate assessment; but surprisingly, the number of similarities between the two are less than one would expect. For instance, Nixon's political career spanned a few decades, whereas, Trump's experience is limited to his tenure in the White House. Nixon was a Navy veteran, while Trump successfully dodged the Vietnam draft with a medical waiver. In addition to this, Trump's apparent ill-regard for the military is evident in a number of comments that he made in recent years. Perhaps the most disheartening comment was related to former Senator John McCain and his experience as a POW during the Vietnam war. According to Trump, "only losers are captured". To date, Trump is the only President who lacks either military or public service prior to becoming President of the United States.

In spite of the numerous dissimilarities, the old adage, "imitation is the best form of flattery", appears to be applicable with Trump and his predecessors. This is particularly true with regard to Trump's usage of euphemistic symbolism and phrases to appeal to the Republican base. For example, the "law and order" phrase that is commonly used by Trump was taken directly from Nixon's political jargon during the race riots in the late 60's. In addition to Trump's use of Nixon's euphemistic symbolism, his overtly racist comments and refusal to denounce the support of White supremacists is reminiscent of Goldwater's approach to the Southern Strategy. Perhaps the most defining similarity to Nixon is the corruption surrounding their respective election campaigns, which resulted in a near-impeachment for Nixon and an impeachment for Trump. Though short lived due to the Watergate Scandal, Nixon's second run for office ended with a landslide win. In contrast; as the country struggles to overcome the effects of the COVID-19 pandemic, a bad economy and rampant racial unrest, Trump's re-election looms in the balance.

The one characteristic that is unique to Donald Trump is his pseudo-concern for African Americans. Public displays of kindness toward African Americans are woven throughout Trump's first term. Along with these very public displays of altruism are overt gestures that strongly promote the actions of White supremacists. In 2016, he received roughly 6%-8% of the African American vote. In a recent poll, 8 in 10 African Americans described him as racist. Based on these findings, Trump is not expected to improve his standing among African Americans during the 2020 election. Again, **the African American vote is not a priority for the Republican Party during Presidential elections**—so why does he waste time creating an illusion of empathy for African American voters? One writer suggests the following:

"These performances are for his supporters, releasing them from any guilt they might harbor over the bigotry Trump spews and giving them the moral authority to claim that they stand for inclusivity".
Dahleen Glanton—Tribune News Service

In the author's opinion—*the pseudo-concern for African Americans is an attempt to become more favorable among African Americans than his predecessor…perhaps another indication of his apparent obsession with President Obama.* In addition to this, his actions may be an attempt to deploy an age-old tactic—divide and conquer—for political gain. This tactic is responsible for the defeat of some of the world's greatest powers.

African American Voters

In the aftermath of the Civil War, the Fourteenth Amendment to the Constitution granted citizenship to the former enslaved; however, it did not guarantee the right to vote. African American voters remained disenfranchised as they were systematically denied the right to vote. The Fifteenth Amendment, which was passed in 1870, was passed to address the issue,

"The right of citizens of the United States to vote shall not be denied or abridged by the United States or by any state on account of race, color, or previous condition of servitude".

Unfortunately, the measure would fail to mitigate the issue, due to the implementation of deterrents for African American voters, to include poll taxes literacy tests, fraud and intimidation. Between 1895 and 1910, Alabama, Georgia, Louisiana, North Carolina, Oklahoma and Virginia implemented the *Grandfather Clause* to further limit the number of African American voters. According to the clause, individuals who were able to vote in 1866 or 1867 and their descendants were exempt from educational, poll taxes or other tax requirements for voting. Since the Fifteenth Amendment was adopted in 1870, the clause effectively excluded African Americans from voting, while assuring that impoverished and illiterate White voters would not be excluded. In 1915, the Supreme Court ruled that it was unconstitutional for states to use the Grandfather Clause to exempt literacy testing for White voters. Without the clause, tens of thousands of poor Southern Whites were disenfranchised along with African Americans. African Americans remained disenfranchised until the passage of the Voting Rights Act of 1965 which provided substantial protection for African American voters for the first time.

THE TWO-PARTY SYSTEM

"The danger of the Republican party being taken over by the lily-white conservatives is more serious than many people realize."
Jackie Robinson, 1963

The two-party system, which is racially polarized, has resulted in a second wave of disenfranchisement for African Americans, an outcome that was predicted by the late Jackie Robinson in 1963. A long time Republican, Robinson's comment was prompted by Senator Goldwater's rise within the party and subsequent nomination for President in 1964. During the Republican National Convention in 1964, African American Republicans were spat on and verbally abused to the point where they believed their lives were in danger. After Goldwater's nomination, Robinson stated,

"It is a new breed which is seeking to sell to Americans a doctrine which is as old as mankind—the doctrine of racial division, the doctrine of racial prejudice, the doctrine of white supremacy."

On the national level (presidential elections) Republicans can easily win elections without the African American vote. As a result, African American initiatives are not a priority for Republican candidates. This dynamic has placed the African American voter at the mercy of the Democratic Party and the one-party system that Jackie Robinson feared. This, in and of itself, is the basis for Trump's assertion that African Americans are "blind Democrats".

Within the one-party system, the greatest disadvantage for African Americans is the fact that the Democratic Party can count on our votes without being held accountable for their actions or inactions on our behalf. For example, Jimmy Carter and Bill Clinton received eighty percent of the African American vote during their first elections. In return, Jimmy Cater distanced himself from policies that would disproportionately benefit African Americans. In contrast, Clinton actually implemented policies that disproportionately impacted African Americans in negative manner. Carter lost his second bid for the White House. Clinton prevailed in his 1996 re-election; in spite of the 1994 Crime Bill, which disproportionately sent thousands of African Americans to prison.

An Overview of the Political Process
To fully understand the importance of voting at all levels of government, a functional understanding of each branch is vital.

The Constitution created the 3 branches of government to ensure a balance of power:
- The **Legislative Branch** (Congress) to make the laws: Senate and the House of Representatives.
- The **Executive Branch** (President of the United States)to enforce the laws.
- The **Judicial Branch** to interpret the laws. The Judicial Branch is a system of federal courts and judges that interpret the laws made by the Legislative Branch. The highest court within the Judicial Branch is the **Supreme Court.**

The President of the United States is the head of the executive branch of government in America. Under Article II of the Constitution, the President is responsible for the execution and enforcement of *laws created by Congress*. While the President has the power either to sign legislation into law or to veto bills enacted by Congress, Congress may in turn override a veto or legislation with a two-thirds vote of both houses (House of Representatives and the Senate).

With regard to executive orders, which give the President the authority to 'clarify or further existing laws' *in the absence of support from Congress*, the power is not absolute. Executive orders are subject to judicial review and may be overturned. Judicial review is a Constitutional measure that ensures the separation of powers between the legislative (Congress) and executive (President of the United States) branches when the latter exceed their authority. Supreme Court Justices, court of appeals judges, and district court judges are nominated by the President and confirmed by the United States Senate, as stated in the Constitution. Because of the role of judicial review in the balancing of power, the appropriate selection of Federal and Supreme Court Judges is crucial...going a step further, Senate races are equally important due to its role in the confirmation process.

The take home message is clear—we can't just vote in Presidential elections and expect the system to work in our favor.

Roles of the House of Representatives and the Senate

Article 1 of the Constitution states, "All legislative Powers herein granted shall be vested in a Congress of the United States, which shall consist of a Senate and House of Representatives." The legislative process is not functional without the consent of both entities. In general, **The House** has several powers assigned exclusively to it, including the power to initiate revenue bills, impeach federal officials, and elect the President in the case of an electoral college tie. **The Senate** has the sole power to confirm those of the President's appointments that require consent, and to ratify treaties. With specific regard to lawmaking, laws begin in the House of Representatives. Once approved in the House, the bill is then sent to the Senate for review. Once approved by the Senate the bill is eventually sent to the President to approve or veto.

Partisanship versus Bipartanship

Regarding the office the Presidency, "the absence of bipartisanship is akin to a soldier having a weapon without ammunition..."

A.L. Smith, Author

Bipartisanship is defined by congressional periods of productive cooperation and compromise between political parties. Partisanship occurs during periods of political polarization. The periods preceding the Civil War and post-Civil War are perhaps the most polarized periods in America's history. In recent American history, the election of President Barack Obama is another example of extreme congressional partisanship. Upon his election in 2008, the House of Representatives and the Senate was led by the Democratic Party. During the first two years of his administration, President Obama was able to pass some key legislative measures, to include the Affordable Care Act, the American Recovery and Reinvestment Act, and Wall Street Reform due to the Democratic majority in both the House and the Senate. In the aftermath of the midterm elections in 2010, the Republicans gained control of the House, with the Democrats maintaining control of the Senate. In 2010, Senate Republican leader Mitch McConnell of Kentucky famously declared that ***the "single most important thing" for the GOP was to make President Obama a one-term president.*** While McConnell was unable to accomplish this goal, gerrymandering and other forms of electoral manipulations created a polarized congress. Republicans adopted a simple, systematic plan to resist anything President Obama proposed. ***"If he was for it,"*** *said former Ohio Senator George Voinovich,* ***"we had to be against it."***

No Republican Senators or House Republicans voted for the Affordable Care Act. The resultant effect of the unified plan to oppose President Obama was profound **nearly all of President Obama's major accomplishments resulted from party-line votes or executive actions.**

In the aftermath of President Obama's administration, some African Americans have been critical of his inability to address certain African American initiatives. One of the goals of this work is to enhance the working knowledge of the political process among African American voters, while emphasizing the importance of our participation in not only Presidential elections, but also Congressional elections and elections on the local and state level. Whereas African Americans responded in record numbers to elect President Obama in 2008 and 2012, we literally "left him hanging" during the mid-term elections in 2010. To be absolutely clear, the lack of bipartisanship during President Obama's tenure is the primary cause of his limited ability to address many of the issues concerning African Americans. With further regard to the power of the Presidency—in the author's opinion, **the absence of bipartisanship is akin to a soldier having a weapon without ammunition...**

CLOSING THE ECONOMIC GAP—ONE POLICY AT A TIME

"I've come upon something that disturbs me deeply...We have fought hard and long for integration, as I believe we should have, and I know that we will win. But I've come to believe we're integrating into a burning house...Until we commit ourselves to ensuring that the underclass is given justice and opportunity, we will continue to perpetuate the anger and violence that tears at the soul of this nation." **Dr. Martin Luther King**

After the emancipation of the enslaved in 1865, General Sherman asked a number of former slaves what was needed to build their lives as freedmen. A minister in the group stated ***"the best way to take care of ourselves is to have land..."***

Special Field Order #15 was issued to allocate hundreds of thousands acres of land so that each family would receive forty acres and a mule. Lincoln signed the measure into law two days before his inauguration. Unfortunately, his assassination and the subsequent placement of Andrew Johnson in charge of Reconstruction would completely alter the measure. Claims of reverse discrimination against Whites resulted in the removal of African American families from the land that had been provided. Sharecropping; which was a continuation of slavery and free labor, became the only option for survival. The end result was the creation of wealth for White Americans and generational poverty for African Americans. For the next 100 years, integration and other social initiatives would dominate the political agenda for African Americans, as the economic gap steadily increased. Dr. King acknowledged the error of the strategy shortly before his death in 1968. In essence, while we were fighting for the right to eat and congregate together, our primary focus should have been economics.

So where do we go from here?

AFRICAN AMERICANS AND THE DEMOCRATIC PARTY

Since the 3/5 Compromise, African Americans have impacted the establishment of political power, but without real benefit. The two-party system that evolved after Emancipation has failed African Americans and the overall impact is resounding. The GOP's purposeful exclusion of African Americans from their political agenda is well-known. However, the concomitant impassiveness and sense of entitlement from the Democratic Party has created a one party system for African Americans—one that should *ideally* address the socioeconomic concerns and overall well-being of African Americans, **considering the fact that the Democratic Party has not won a Presidential election without the African American vote since World War II.**

In spite of this, issues that disproportionately impact African Americans continue to be ignored by elected officials. The impassiveness of the Democratic Party over the years has resulted in the disenfranchisement and subsequent indifference to the political system among African Americans—particularly among young African Americans. The 2016 Presidential election is an important demonstration of the impact. Because of the relationship with the Republican Party and the lack of enthusiasm for Hilary Clinton, an overwhelming number of African Americans opted to forgo participation completely. As a result, Donald

Trump is now the 45th President.

Clearly, the impact of the African American vote is undeniable —**especially when cast with unity. This is particularly true on the state level.** For further emphasis—too often, African American voters are compelled to participate in presidential elections, while failing to participate on the local and state level. This practice has failed us time and time again as evidenced by the impact of the midterm elections and ensuing partisanship that occurred during President Obama's administration. To demonstrate the impact of the African American vote on the state level, the 2017 Senate race in Alabama is perhaps one of the best examples. Alabama is a prototypical "Confederate State" where remnants of the Old South remain strong. Prior to the realignment of parties in the 1960s, conservative, "Old South", voters remained loyal to the Democratic Party. This was in spite of the increasing number of African American Democrats. Since the implementation of the Southern Strategy, the Republican Party of Alabama has dominated the political scene for several decades. In fact, prior to 2017, a Democrat hadn't held a Senate seat in Alabama since 1992. In the 2017 Senate race, Republican candidate Roy Moore was projected to win the election against Democrat Doug Jones in spite of the scandal that emerged against Roy Moore during the campaign. Such was not the case. Doug Jones managed to unseat the incumbent Republican, and **his win was based on the fact that 96% of the African American vote** was cast in support of the Democratic Candidate, Doug Jones. This election is a demonstration of power and unity in its purest form and should be the blue print for African Americans in the re-strategizing of our political position as stakeholders in the political process, as opposed to simply **"blind Democrats"** as Trump so eloquently implied. An emphasis on the importance of voting is the first step in actualizing the change that we seek. The second step is demanding accountability in exchange for our votes.

In the spirit of Dr. King... the ultimate goal of the African American voter should be the achievement of economic equality and the closing of the economic gap—one policy at a time.

 r. A.L. Smith read her first full-length novel (The Boxcar Children, by Gertrude Chandler Warner) in the third grade and it spawned her passion for reading. According to Dr. Smith, the hallmark of a great story is the resounding presence of a character that transcends the final pages of the book.

Dr. Smith is a native of Frierson, Louisiana. She attended Grambling State University on a basketball scholarship and later joined the school's Army ROTC program. Upon graduation in 1996, she became the university's first Army ROTC cadet to receive a commission in the Army Nurse Corps and was recently promoted to the rank of Lieutenant Colonel in the Army Reserves. Dr. Smith is a practicing Certified Registered Nurse Anesthetist with a Doctorate of Nurse Anesthesia Practice degree from Texas Wesleyan University. Her research study was selected for publication in the 2016 edition of the Journal of Gastroenterology Nursing issue 39 volume 2.

Dr. Smith is an Amazon Best Selling author, an award-winning independent filmmaker and founder of POWER, Inc., a 501 (c)(3) non-profit organization that is dedicated to the reduction of juvenile delinquency through the creation of artistic content and curricula that enlightens, inspires and emPOWERS underprivileged and at-risk youth. In 2010, she participated in humanitarian relief efforts during the devastating earthquake in Haiti and provided anesthesia services to a countless number of victims, many of whom were children. This experience would have a profound impact on her views concerning socioeconomic disparities here in the U.S. and countries abroad. Her second novel, Behind Closed Doors 2: Dana's Story, was heavily influenced by her experience in Haiti.

Dr. Smith is a member of Alpha Kappa Alpha Sorority, Inc. and takes seriously the organization's motto "Service to all Mankind".

Her personal motto is *"In as much as you've done to the least of the..."*

.

www.ingramcontent.com/pod-product-compliance
Lightning Source LLC
Chambersburg PA
CBHW050800240726